The Luster of Everything I'm Already Forgetting

The Luster of Everything I'm Already Forgetting

Poems by

Nicole Rollender

Dear Laurie,

Every night when we go to sleep, one world ends... but a new one starts for us at first daylight. I hope you find what resonates in these poems.

Cheers,

Cover design by Shay Culligan
Cover image, *The Nativity,* 1858, by Arthur Hughes,
Birmingham Museum and Art Gallery
Author photo by Rick Urbanowski

ISBN: 978-1-63980-350-7

Kelsay Books
502 South 1040 East, A-119
American Fork, Utah 84003
Kelsaybooks.com

For Grant, Grace, and Zachary,
always and again

.

Acknowledgments

Poems in this manuscript have appeared in the following journals:

Amethyst Review: "Locution I: We are more wretched than the animals"

The American Poetry Journal: "If I Could Have Been Born the Lord's Dog," "A Body's a Difficult Thing"

The Baltimore Review: "A Dream of My Father Walking on Water, After Deciding to Burn His Childhood Photos"

Bearings Online: "Meditation Excerpt: Annunciation"

The Bellingham Review: "I Still Don't Believe in the Beauty of Forgiveness"

Birdcoat Quarterly: "Locution V: He is the law of crows," "Locution VI: Bleeding is burning is survival"

Calla Press: "Arrangement of Desire," "Locution II: This is a love that kills"

Clayjar Review: "Locutions"

dialogist: "Tell Me How You Understand Vanishing Point"

Diode Poetry Journal: "Ways of Blessing," "Notes: Gratitude for Still Being Alive"

Ekstasis: "After Not Drinking Anymore"

Lake Effect: "You Can't See Ghosts"

MockingHeart Review: "The Etymology of Poltergeist"

The Night Heron Barks: "Recurring Dreams as Lazarus"

Ninth Letter: "Why I Carry Guilt as a Lantern"

Open: Journal of Arts & Letters: "Yesterday's Gutted Girl," "The Etymology of Sacrifice"

The Other Journal: "Meditation Excerpt: Mater Dolorosa," "Meditation Excerpt: Change Me, O Ghost"

Palette Poetry: First place winner of the 2019 Previously Published Prize, "The Luster of Everything I'm Already Forgetting." Originally published in *Gigantic Sequins,* and winner of the journal's sixth annual poetry contest.

Parabola VOL. 42:4 Families: Winner of 2017 Thomas Mertens Poetry of the Sacred Contest, Center for Interfaith Relations, "How I Learned to Pray"

Presence: Pushcart Prize nominee 2018, "How I Learned to Forgive a Good Man"

Puerto Del Sol: "Novena for When My Son Doesn't Want to See Spirits"

Tinderbox Poetry Journal: "Sorrow Singing"

Typishly: "Residual Memory of Mercy"

Radar Poetry: Finalist for 2017 Coniston Poetry Prize, "Lamp Lighting," "Holy Fools Day Litany," "Lost Things Keep Appearing," "Littlest Bones," "Threshold with a Crown of Bees"

Red Paint Hill: "My Grandmother Carried Me as Kindling"

The Shore: "Grow to Love the Vanishing," "Noctuary"

Sky Island Journal: "Diverging"

Superstition Review: "Empty Church"

Thrush Poetry Journal: "In the Silence After the Other Driver T-Boned Our Car, I Looked in the Rearview Mirror to See if My Children Were Still Alive," "Morning Prayer"

trampset: "Litany with Outpouring Light"

Verse-Virtual: "Little Candle in the Coming Rain," "Lux Brumalis," "Lux Aeterna"

Vox Viola: "Story I Tell in the Dark When I Can't Sleep," "Grief Constellation"

Contents

Part III

Part IV

Part V

Ways of Blessing

Holy nomenclature   of firetipped butterflies shining   holy my wet
orchard of abandoned belongings   let me feed the needy
with fruit   at least unlatch

my tongue & feed it to a child   afraid to name the world
the heart doesn't run the body   any time the ghost

can unknot from its mooring   eternity & grief both look like water
bless blue-cold midnight   when we light lanterns

from this hearth's fire   when God's deathless face compasses
us from darkness to never-failing flame   when I was a girl, I ate meals

separate from my parents so they could talk   holy that loneliness
that hasn't left me   holy fence broken through   where we see sheep's

breath   the color of rotting blossoms   we choose to bless
or curse to call goodness or evil   our worst suffering

is no more serious than one night in an unlighted motel   a bat's
leg bones are so thin   it cannot walk

it seems unfair   too, the mother who doesn't know to finger
the sign of the cross on her sleeping child   not entering

paradise by the precision of just one hair's breakage   but you can't
kneel in your future beside the fence

you'll build   post holes filling with rain   the holes I left
in my mother's bones & the glow   in her marrow bless

beeswax candles at the moment of sacrifice   bless this bed's wood
this down   shall we have many children here (the gate

to heaven where my husband cups my shoulders)   where my body
houses another body   I have two names   I'm glad for late-
daylight

rusting my skin   that I can still touch someone else   open my
body to a girl child   unmoor her sleep body   holy

her fistfuls of wings   holy her life after mine

Part I

O my God, what am I / That these late mouths /
should cry open / In a forest of frost, in a dawn of cornflowers?
—Sylvia Plath

Threshold with a Crown of Bees

Love doesn't want this body. A sparrow's in the tree,
then he's gone—chasing steeples.

In black-and-white photos of an old
apiary, bees crown
the keeper's head, sugary swarm,

blur of graying flight I imagine the third
child I'm homesick

for (the one I never had) lives as—motherless in a cold
cove, nameless in a garden of stars.
Like my mother's humming—*aren't*

there sparrows left? There aren't any sparrows left.
When I dust my daughter's dollhouse,

painted bougainvillea on pink walls—soon, she'll cast
it away. When another child suicide bomber blows
up by remote control. Tell me,

is there a different word (or world)
for light or lonely in the darkening? Is

light ever alone? Tell me there's a man somewhere
weighting a calf's neck, submerging its wild
kicking, sobbing under the river water.

The collar bells singing memories
I've never lived—this child drawing a bee,

calling it treasure-body's honey thrum.
Somewhere in the world you might be knifed
for what moves inside you—it's true, the human
body gives off an imperceptible glow.

The moon slides. Never-ending night, a black
horse kneels at the field's edge.

How I Learned to Pray

God dwells among the pots and pans.
　　　　　　　　—St. Teresa of Avila

God dwells among the pots　　& pans, I learned　　　the hard way
Grandmother's kitchen toil　　to save electricity, oil lamps

hands' litany　　in suds　how inconsequential to scrape
chicken grease with my nails　　each plate & tine　a reminder we

fed the family　tooth grind & heel

Grandmother's ladle clanging　gravy boat, iron hooves　on the roof
on clouds　　we're always readying the body　to travel toward

another life　Grandmother could see the dead　& yellow & plum
lights off the living　The things a body can be　boated spices

queen bee's spilled wreckage　oubliette

or a pear's womb opening　My daughter & I visited a chapel
the host the color　of barley　of pilgrim knees　cross debossed

in parchment　its center's outglowing　Candles surrounding
maybe God pitying my weak will　maybe the fleecy

differences between　what

you remember & what's there　my father　guarding my door
against night　spirits who walk　or not, it's the thought

that comforts   makes me believe

I'm worth saving   My father had a holy water   beginning, river
baptism   what a mercy to start over   What a mercy

I haven't had   What mercy we can give   when our baby
son steps   on a toad smaller than a penny   when he realizes

he has killed   one boned world,   we can give   him another

Meditation Excerpt: Annunciation

One of Ireland's abandoned cloisters. Elsewhere, whitethorn wound around a martyr's head reliquary. Be still, wildflowers at its center, rising claret sky its impossible nave. Burning yews, I walked into its feral stone, my life a shipwreck when I was 16: What I want is still always the same, to change my life. Mary's *yes*, after the archangel asked, his opulent shadows. How do you live in this world after all of heaven says *yes* back? Wounds of grace, we're dying of love in strawberries' gleam. Yet again, watching a hummingbird's tension. Hovering—crimson incandescent gorget—God's perfect machine. Sapphire smokelight. She said *yes*— gilded dart a joyful prayer—to watch her son die. What do you shape from terror? In my blackout nights when I didn't know God, the pieces assembled as heifers slow-moving in a herd of breath. My heart turning as my premature son jostles in his crib. Light on my tongue: foreshadow, forsake & unbind, but heaven starts in the mind—earth's not our home— illumined & charred. The heart moves & moves again.

Why I Carry Guilt as a Lantern

In late thistle-spine summer, cicadas belled in the yard. This lavender
light an incomplete

apology. I wasn't a virgin sewing layettes (or my own shroud) in the
museum half-light. I fell

asleep husked in my grandmother's trunk on sun-bleached doilies
dreaming her ghost

scaled my spine. I found my box of baby teeth, then rebuilt tiny jaws
on a windowsill. My mother sang

about archangels dancing in my molar crevices—I was happy she
remembered me by my bones &

> I found a cemetery washed away in marigolds & named longing,
> girdles & red paper

birds. The sky was a girl fast-walking from the baby's breath where
the dog & I stopped

—the next morning my father put her to sleep, & I couldn't stop him.

I prayed (another apology) to the Black Madonna—surely, she knew
how to search for me. I lived

with my grandmother's urn. Where's the place our voices go after the
body burns? My son

will always ask, *Mama, mama, is your name still inside you?*
He knows

now how dark it is inside his ribs. At dusk a flock will rise & scatter
again, arrowed Hail Marys

flung toward any mother who'll listen. I sing my son lullabies & leave the light

on so he'll fall asleep. Will I ever tell him how my mother found the paring knife in my room

& let me choose whether to keep it?

The Luster of Everything I'm Already Forgetting

I press my mouth   to my son's warm back,   cowbells distant.
This wild   longing to keep   my body between his   & any kind
of desolation.   Sharp-boned spells   to ripen baskets   of Old World
potatoes & Christ's body   on my tongue: Make me
a good mother.   A woman photographed a polar   bear dragging
a cub's head   across snow, tendons' red   wreckage the color
of earth after it's burned   or how fireflies' light looks   after you've
smashed 100   bodies to pulp   a still shimmer   of survival.
The doctor cut   my perineum   to free my son,   heartbeat
a gallop   galloping—& now   he wants to sleep   standing
like a cow   but I beg him to lay down.   Cows can only dream
on their veined   sides.   I think of the mother bear   if she isn't
dead, how was the cub   taken   unless famine season—   but we
have to fight   to the death, don't we.   My son asks   how he
got out   of my dark body.   I tell him   he was cut free   & he
says he folded   himself like origami   before emerging   a scorpion
razor-tailing out.   When he sleeps, I re-hang   his fallen star map
& trace   his blue crayon trails (Google   says they're lies) over
Eradinus,   heaven's river   its star names catch   my mother
throat: Azha, hatching place   Keid's broken eggshells.   I don't wake
my son to look   at the moon. He sleeps   to grow, while I suture
velvet   hands that care too much   & not enough.   Sad house,
since the cat has gone.   I want answers from these walls   —they've

watched mothers   before me hold   vomiting children   & then

bathe them. This   is the task we're given, stay,   because if you go,

your child   may wander   into a field filled   with rifle fire.

& the origami body   paper-thin skin cleft from yours can ignite:

Flaming wildflower scent   in his matted hair steels   though me.

Once my blue-veined breasts ached   to feed him &   I'm sorry

I can't remember that pain   anymore; how easy it is   to forget

the exactness of certain   blades. & is that   the way the body heals

again   & again before entering the kingdom   of death,   trees

white-garlanded   & the many women carrying water   jugs?

I miss my grandmother   who lost children young   & her

memories of holding them   dead, they were so   luminous, she said,

daylight just gone.   The soul's homeland   nameless. Now,   their

bones all braided together   yellow tulips shake dirt loose.

Empty Church

I used to list my sins,
whispering them in the shower
so I wouldn't forget any stinging
one before confession. When I prayed
my penance, I knelt on the wood floor,
not the padded kneeler, sweet Lord,
I prayed hard, in the desperate way
I did years later in Chartres' astonishing
grayness, where I fit bare knees
into grooves, the marble still here,
yet centuries of pilgrim bones.
I knew I could die at any moment,
lost from grace, but desire kept pinning
me to the bed. My tongue caught
in the world's breath. And because
my voice wasn't made for singing,
I kept my mouth closed, whispered
when we've been there 10,000
years, so only the invisible
& their shining heard me.
Something happens though, after
you birth a child, then two:
Your breasts leak. Your back
heaves from carrying them through
the 3 am nightmare hours. The body
becomes the burden you're sorry for.
I count heartbeats. I trust no one.

Because I know I could die in my sleep,
as could they, I consider what I say
to God now, that I long for copper
flowers in eternity, a house forever
in light, the wind off a river. I watch God
with one eye, as I rock a baby, this loud
body-psalm of need the only holiness I know
now. Yet, my God, who comes as warm bread
on a table, who comes as the radiant day
I wake into—

Lost Time in a Greening Cloister

An October day, now the memory of salt & fromageries in Paris
& wind-dark—

birds the swoops of cathedrals. How bright is death? The thought
of its gallop

makes all things begin again. A bee tangling its feet in wild honey,
the godly

hum of aglow wings. When I imagine my grandmother cocooned
in purgatory,

she swims alone in an empty room of twilight, not knowing how
she got there. A

blackout. Or where a door might open. How easy for her to leave,
eyes rolling

up as Ave Maria floated from the radio. Now, I pray for her release
into heavenly

ether. I'm still here, otherwise, if not for a surrounding grace. If not
for the radiant

eye of my God. If not for thinking death is me actually being born. Then,
that door

cracks. The magenta leaves blowing around our house. The birds
shadowing. The wind.

How easy it is for the next snow to cover my tracks. My mouth a hungry
ghost.

If I Could Have Been Born the Lord's Dog

Wake me in the feverish / ship's cabin, wake me / my Old World
forehead / gilded with the third eye. / My first boy sleeping / sticky
bread in his palm / holy mother pollinating / holy child. My sorrow
songs / *zal dusze sciska,* / clutching my soul / *serce bolesc czuje* / my
painful heart / make me younger / forget I'll never / see my mother
again. / My husband landlocked / in Jersey City stocking / our brown
stone / with second-hand pots / & spoons. Orchards / where I blessed
branches to bloom fruit / left behind in Płock / meadows gypsies
crossed & sharp- / bladed spells to ripen / baskets of potatoes / ancient
dust body of Christ—soil / my body won't enter. / My husband doesn't
speak the language / of America, so how will I? / Still, I spin the future.
I see through crypt / walls, saints glowing / over their own soot / & lace-
worked bones / & more mothers / offering another's son / to the lion,
to the evil eye. / I was a village dweller. / No one opened / their door
to me. / My namesake, Domenic, whose mother / dreamed him / a dog
leaping / from her womb / a torch in his mouth. / If I could / have set
the world / on fire. If / I was born / the Lord's dog. / I touch my boy's
cheek, singing / *Sto lat, sto lat / niech żyje, żyje nam.* / May you live
100 birthdays. / Are you asking / why such grief / that I see others'
deaths / coming, but not my own? / My son's heart / will stop when
he's 40. / His wife locks / him out / of the house. / Hex. The beauty
of that dark hole. / My son. I'll sit / in the oak / chair my husband
carpenters for me now / my son's spirit hand / rocking me
instructing / there's a devil in me / that's not me.

Sorrow Singing

O, hip bone (yours) over thigh bone (mine) buttressing (cathedral-
body night)
what we can't keep out.
We won't gate it

(any longer): this pink bird of thundering (sometimes gorgeous),
the beast undoing
what we've made: (a marriage
in gossamer).

I never told you my great-grandmother stopped attending church. Our
daughter sings
doxology at
her window (open) so

the neighbors hear her glory. Two nuns forced her (my grandmother)
to hit her brother
over and over
in front of the class

red marks burning (now) into all our arms. *Sicut erat in principio,*
when the word became
flesh, the ghosted holy

over, *et nunc,* my plague-masked face (the woman you see), *et semper,*
if we can
unbless (our union)
make it newly feathered,

et in saecula saeculorum, (which world) any place we feel alive again,
our skin
unharmed by wind
by flame, by living (hand).

Channeling

Put these words in a leather bag / walnut cutting / sound of wind
the first person / you see after you leave / your house the one
who eats worms dancing / to overcome melancholia / such
an unhappy fate / what I needed was absolution / the priest's sign
of the cross / over me so / many times that's how I'd sleep / arms
outstretched into a ship / mast waiting for nails / you can't take
the wild out / of this girl who hexes / is hexed / I pray to the Virgin
I cradle her dolors / I throw salt over / the left, always the left
shoulder, wish for stigmata / glass perfume decanters / of holy
water and throat brooches / black hair that untangles / in two
curtains at night / down the back / flogged by / we're going
to the lighthouse / we are / the light / sent over the sea / undersea
the ship I came on / sinking boat / constellations' broken teeth
dried thyme & sorrow / I carry recipes / for peasant bone broth
that carries oxen clod & tail / potato deep from the earth / my
black skirt full of rain / my mother finds stains on my sheets
she won't tell me / I'm not dying / she won't / tell me the girl
she was / the girl who fed chickens / the girl I am / sent away at 8
to another farm to work / soles worn to holes / arch-scarred
chickens' mouths / dark-pitched woman / I see in the mirror
a cross in one / hand / the evil eye inked / on the other / thresh-
holded women / behold the lamb / of slaughter / of God behold.

The Etymology of Sacrifice

*(v) To offer something to a deity as an expression of thanks,
devotion or penitence*

My son asked if I could have given him for adoption—
or offered him to be cut in half to satisfy another mother.
When I turned my body over to grow his, I didn't expect
the bleeding or broken placenta that cast him out nine weeks
early. But those stars shining over me then are the same ones
silently watching now. One day his childhood will end. One
day I'll become part of his past. If one of us dies, we're still
alive in a smartphone: us laughing in our fireball red Trans
Am, a firebird flying through the Pine Barrens. We're laughing
over "Paradise City," the wind pulling my black & purple hair
through open T-tops. He's a little boy who understands the cross,
but still expects to be happy. God, how could you turn your son
over to this world?

The Etymology of Poltergeist

(n.) A noisy spirit who makes its presence known by noises or knockings

My firstborn, 3 lbs. 17 oz., in a hospital incubator with a strawberry birthmark over her right eye. I sat by her. I held her, saying, *Come home. Stay with me.* She won't remember my singing, my dead grandmother singing to her. Blackbirds cackling in a witness tree. From German, literally a "noisy ghost," from *poltern*, "to rattle": The wine bottles I hid under the bed clanking as I lay face down above, not unlike a snow angel. Sleepwalking. My body emptied of a baby. Haunted rooms. She took more than 10 seconds to cry, a fire in the rain. The act of naming her: saint, stone, sainted stone, saint almost drowned by a stone tied around her middle, but for stunning graces. So, Grace. Birthmarked. Descendent of angels. Birds thundering in my nightmares. Mouthful of bones in lucid dreams. Of hens running from the hatchet. Men sailing toward earth's edge where oceans drop off into eternity. This baby, tiny kite I barely hold, disappearing up into spectral skies. Silverware clinking in a diner, crucifix lighting up my neck. While she slept in the incubator, my father asked why I wouldn't eat the turkey or mashed potatoes. Humming, buzzing, tinny rattling a wishbone I can't crack. A *poltern* crossing stepping stones in my gut. Dear baby, dear stranger, I didn't know I'd want your immensity tying me to this world. I knelt by the river rattling nightly. Your ship carried me.

My Grandmother Carried Me as Kindling

My grandmother carried me
as kindling, her mother
                          tongue hard to taste.
Her stories didn't tell how her daughters
died
                          (I imagined that myself in night's

cold countryside).
In my grandmother's night-tales,
always a briar tangle
                          & a girl (a flower with no scent)

hiding from a woodsman, bird-
trembling in cold branches. Once there were many girls
who hadn't been born
                          & many others who saw death as a gift,

        she'd begin. Stop
                          hungering for the field;

the wind's already empty.
& the man's shadow
shouldering his axe,
                          crosses the girl's shut eyes

(& mine, still). Sometimes, the woodsman
sniffs out the girl (who'll never marry),
                          homesick now for mother's

cabbage soup. He pulls her up
as if to bury her in the sky,
                          cape's scruff a wound

in his hand.
My

                lily, she'd say,

pulling the blanket
up my chest, how you live

                makes the bed you'll sleep in.

Part II

You see, I want a lot. / Maybe I want it all: / the darkness of each endless fall, / the shimmering light of each ascent.
—Rainer Maria Rilke

Recurring Dreams as Lazarus

(i)

outside someone shakes the trees for fruit   the falling isn't beautiful

No, I covet what's inside each fruit   dark seeds   a whole second life

(ii)

a strange short season   I scrub the tomb's floor

a shine so, so Our Lady of the Sea's   blues shimmer, reflecting

(iii)

I contemplate what composes me   shrouded sickbones as flute's fire

seabirds' chant   stench of a pandemic city   but, morning's wet flowers

but, bread, honey   obedience in ash   & milk, lavender

body of the sun

(vi)

you can't die twice   we bury our dead   we come back with oranges

we leave our dead   we leave our dead to keep living   to crown our sons

but, here where   goats wander,   I still have sisters   I remember it all

(v)

sometimes, you're born to be one of God's miracles   a sadness come

to change the world   O holy God, I feel your breath   you float

over me   your unmistakable ghost

Story I Tell in the Dark When I Can't Sleep

Mother of Shined Spoons, Mother of Simmering Soup, my great-
grandmother craved

Chanel No. 5 & amaretto. Across a ravine a wolf opens its mouth:
teeth's gleam a row

of lit candles in front of Our Lady the Morning Star. Haunting Jersey
City's thrift shops,

she hoarded cut-glass decanters, her eyes calm among snows. Still,
veiled women kneel

and incant, *O, our causa salutis,* lead us and our children across
the ocean in glass ships. Let

us float as lace. Seven holes in her heart. Lead us, never sinking.
Her plaster Nativity's quiet

animals' chipped musculatures wrapped in January 1961 newspaper.
Raw-rubbed, they don't

escape the witch's city. Lead us in circles. Lead us, iced saints. Lead
us to ancient baths

to heal our calloused feet. Her brownstone knocked down, but I still
smell darkening tea

leaves, tarnish. Cypress. A foreigner among women who can't conjure,
who can sleep. I

want to tell you I haven't prayed enough lately. I haven't sewn up
my son's stuffed elephant,

its cotton guts spilled near my hope chest.

Arrangement of Desire

The names of my beloveds who aren't returning. A night of blue frost,
high stars. When we went to that tiny Cape Cod, remember the lights
going out? Tinged bird feathers rustling on the sill. No matter how I
make my lists, I can't separate my soul from you. It's easier to imagine
me absent, like the cumbersome branch you removed from the pear
tree—no more ducking. Yet, the old reflex stays, to duck your back
on the way to the shed. Even if I escape the limits of my body, even
if my hand isn't there to find yours in bed, we feel a phantom limb.
Ghost branch heavy with white flowers & spring moths. Blood clot
swirling in the toilet after the test showed two lines. We should accept
we can lose everything. Long bands of light. The first time, us stretching
field into mountain, the beginning of slow, our bodies drift on thick
horses at twilight, green as trapped souls in peat bogs. Your grandfather
dug up the bullet-in-calf bone, in cornfields past the quiet barn—filled
with dust-covered clocks, chair frames, what bird skulls make of wings.
Here, in Gettysburg, the barn found a soldier, his buttons & spoons
intact. We have to be ready to give everything up. Horse chestnuts fallen
on this battlefield. Rusty leaves dampening, deeper by breastworks.
Lord, let them assemble among us. You know how I've knelt by these
stones, forehead on the same gray rock, as if I could be then & now.
I realize I'll go on living, in spite of these sorrows. If God's the sea &
souls eternal stars reflecting. Single bones between rocks, between
speaking their names for the last & always after. Die untethered into.
Golden bleeds. Since I can see the faces of the dead, I've wondered
if I was born a garlanded agent of the supernatural. Someone lingers
between goldenrod & fence, his hand out to a lamb, its mouth opening
to what strange, delicious forb he offers.

Second Sight

Golden pollen, horseshoe & sickle. Old iron stench steamed
to song. Outside a fieldstone & red Gettysburg barn, you mouth,

I'm no one, then hand this fruit-stained bible back to the tour
guide. Left to rot, a barn without its body: in its leaf,

Return to Foster Killingsley's family, if found. A man who's called
missing until world's end. When his raptured bones rise

out of these pastures. When we call ourselves illumined. What you
want is new words for all the old things. No, you want new names

for the same old things. Why can't you wake in your sunlit bed three
decades ago, body clean-pressed as a father's Sunday handkerchiefs?

Your grandparents hadn't yet crossed evening's fields, woolen-haired
trundle toward a far gate. Blowing through a flock of sheep, where we

leave our dead. They're a homeward wind as we're broken. There's
no difference between fairies & angels, your daughter says,

because they all protect her. One day, she might cast away all winged
things, but now they open their mouths and spill lighted sea brine

into her path. Still, you tell yourself your deep blue center isn't—it's
not your mother loving you less than the boys. Naming it something

else doesn't change anything. Or starve it. At night, can you tell your
hand from mine? Your daughter renamed her angel 100 times—Lichen,

Hand of God, Ghost Lion, Tender Friend. You can't tell her yet:
An angel somewhere misses a body—he never walked barefoot

in a misting cornfield. A nail never lodged in his sole.

Residual Memory of Mercy

Everything is the hopesprung phantom
of something else. I married

that man, the next morning for a moment
not knowing why I was tucked

in his bed. He collects spoons'
shiny reserve, clay pots of lush succulents,

handmade soaps smelling of spiced apples &
wet horsehair. He moves through me

as through a quiet house.
As if he has thought what he'll do

when I die.
He says I'm dark fruit.

A wind moving outside myself.
A stone wall with one hole.

Even now, he says he loves me as I
came to him, lopsided limbs he's

accustomed to, my night murmurings
a murder of charcoal crows. He says I sleep

with my mouth overflowing,
as they enter or exit at will.

Grief Constellation

Is it wrong to tell you that my body's in ruins—ruined
     by my bones moving

the seasons? Sometimes, the dead won't believe they're no
     longer alive. When my son stuffed his left

     foot in his right shoe, I gently removed it—he surrendered,
     as I guided his right foot into the sneaker

     that fit. He relaxed in a way the dead can't, luminous
     machinery wavering on the sunlit floor,

forever uncontainable. When they're gone, nothing's
     music, as everything is: fork clattering in the sink, aluminum

     clang a sign, or not. Visiting the Abbaye du Mont-Saint-Michel,
     I always remember a red curtain cloaking

     a nun's window. After we left, she must have watered the
     medieval herb garden. What a grace. Dissolving 1,000

years to a simpler theology: Angelica calms the stomach. Salt
     keeps spirits out. Feverfew calms migraines. Salt

     flavors our meat. The soul's agleam. Salt keeps us afloat.
     If you want eternal rest, my grandmother told me,

sift rosemary under your pillow to banish nightmares. This fall night, the cold's kneeling in the road.

I'm not sure if this strange singing is my body, or the one to come.

Gift

My grandmother clasped cousin Stella's hand, divining the heart

of things: The only house she'd buy would burn in the spring,

daughters' dresses floating through windows. Peculiar sight twining

in our bloodline, yet our bodies trouble to make moon-eyed children.

Is this a hex on my back? I've buried my mother's hallelujahs

& salt-throwing grandmother's prophecies (she said I was in love,

she was wrong) in the sea's dark oil. Still, I touched José's arm.

I saw his mother slap him for pissing on the floor. He hated me for it.

The third eye's gate swings open, letting visions in & out as horses.

I asked my grandmother, who baked doughy babka & lifted her hands'

glowing bones to make the sign of the cross, who do you watch?

Now, she's gone & I'm lonely, knowing all bright things pass away.

On the other side, women laboring in the saint-fields grow younger,

she told me, touching chin whiskers. Here, I carry others' lives,

incessant bird-noise suffering. I split myself over & over, then sew

these little deaths inside my pelvis. I cry to be carried. Because we all

long for something to quiet us down. *Tell me,* the living & dead say,

you'll see me even when my ashes blow away. Out of my skull, evening

primrose will flower. Out of the wildest dark.

Holy Fools Day Litany

When
my daughter asks
if I'll remember

     this twilight, purpling leaves lacing
     her hair, cricket
     murmur, I can't say: You don't know
     what you're asking. No,

     this is my failing—
     soon I won't recall

the day-ending light's shift
on your face bones,

here, now. I've forgotten
to buy you a new
toothbrush again. The search
for God, *he sounds*

     like stars, she says, is deadly—
     which is more brutal,
     to enter him
     & be entered, or to enter

     & be changed forever? Coming
     back through this door

(she uncoiled
my body) after tasting

the Lord makes a person
skittish—you unhinge: sleep
in a tub, eat
bread baked on cow

      dung, drink dish
      water, carry an ever-
      lit lamp searching
      for just one honest

      person. How St. Xenia wore her husband's
      name & clothing
      after he died, sleeping
      in a field to keep

him alive. How the search for my daughter's
doll ended
in finding only the tiny
silken slippers

      under a bush. We believe
      the earth's made just for us.
      Then, it shatters.

God bless the dead's
ecstatic nestle

      in rain's
      choir
      —how fool am I for lifting

my moon-eyed daughter
away from an earth

where maggots clean
a felled fawn's

skull among lilies, excising
a wound
from the inside out? Where my body
also unburdened—

sliding out my blood-
bodied firstborn,
love's glisten.
Where we live among

everything that's dying,
where I still begin the poem again.

Child fit in my hip
bones, she's the wildflower I float
in water, small saint ripping
each petal from the stalk

with her teeth.

Meditation Excerpt: My Daughter as Small Saint

I expect a bird's litany to dislodge from her mouth. Her unpainted instrument for what is, is not the truth. We can't unsee the dead. Still, we reattach hissing wing bones to our scapula. This is the oldest part of the cemetery, then, this snow dripping in bone yards, bones, glint on bones. I watch petals bloom from her mouth into a perpetual spine-sawing song— you can't survive on bread, light & glass alone. I've wondered if I can live without longing now, for all I haven't done & may never. Let her sleep curled with a spotted rabbit we didn't bring home from the fair. We used to believe the uterus roamed through the body, red-sweating. Wherever it braced, the woman clutched her pain. Lord, what a fire at the base of my skull as I learn mothering. When her head crowned, I reached to pull her out, heart erratic as lightning. Now, she pulls my soul *so* through my body, red thread through the needle's eye. I called her *my grace,* meaning I thought I was barren, yet I grew a small cathedral. The first time I saw her face tinged with ice & blueberries, eyes sewn shut, it was the first time I saw the world—my daughter crossing my borders naked, nothing in her tiny hands. Yet her phantom breath stays inside me—an echo, disappearing ink, a snowflake growing smaller as it's cut out and out from parchment. & my words stuck in her throat—

You Can't See Ghosts

You can't imagine how many times my parents used that line on me. Yes, an old couple lived in this ivy-covered split before us. Yes, they died, but they don't sit next to your bed whispering like gyroscopes. Even if you could see the man's black eyes, heavy brow and hawkish nose, he wasn't really there, though the darkness congealed in his wrinkles. The dead don't let you forget them, like Uncle Ziggy sitting in his leather armchair when we got back from his funeral. (Remember when I triumphantly yelled, "Uncle Z beat the Grim Reaper!" and you dragged me from the brownstone?) Or Old Papa John, who didn't realize he crossed over for a while & couldn't find the light switch? Or Aunt Blanche, whose ashes sat on a dresser next to her Lenox swan for two years waiting to be buried, while she'd show up red-eyed & pissed off? Or Uncle Ken, who everyone called "a good man, gone too soon, too fast," passing by with an eagle-winged

spirit? But, remember, none of this is real & you can't see ghosts. Because the spirit's locked up like a little beating hummingbird clock next to the spleen & when it's released, it's gone. A puff. A snow squall. A poof of Grandpa's cigar (he also came back, jaunty stepped, from purgatory on his way to paradise). But you can't see ghosts, especially not the ones who die by suicide. Not the clothing designer who sublimated Baroque art onto silk scarves & called you at work, raving about damaged hearts & getting angry when you hung up. And you didn't have that dream three nights in a row where he put a gun to his head in a garage & pulled the trigger. (Though it's true, on the third morning his sister called to say he shot himself in the head in his garage & he died.) The problem is, your Eternal

Rests can't help him now, unless he wasn't in his right mind. The death-by-hangings are among the most tormented & they want to show you how they looped the rope

around their warm necks. The what-if moment in between kicking away the chair & not. Sometimes they regret it. Sometimes they don't. Sometimes during a Halloween party, they show you how they did it in the attic. They squeeze a length of rope around their own neck so hard it burns yours. Sometimes, the homeowner says, "Yes, the former tenant did hang himself. We didn't want anyone to know." But the secret's out. They tell you where you can visit his grave. And you still can't see ghosts. But sometimes, this is the night your husband says, "That's it," & converts, taking the Confirmation name George, for the saint who slayed the dragons that everyone says aren't real & you can't see.

A Body's a Difficult Thing

Pregnant with ghost / stories, a body / bewilders, such a difficult
merciless thing to keep / Aunt Cin's dried white / wedding irises hang
bound upside- / down in the walk- / up attic, inverse to how / she

died. Icy / kaleidoscope / of butterflies / blued wings / pianist's
finger veins / collapsed in a freak / frost's sugar ice. / Elsewhere, heart
of sparrows. / Parsnips. Wine. A little girl, / all match stick arms / &

legs, chases her mother / dark little chariot / both knowing / always
she didn't want a child. / Plain as her hands / printed on a steamed-up
mirror. / *I'm here. I'm here.* / Once a grandmother said / if you stand

at the top of the stairs / when it's dark / a ghost will push you. / Radiant
choir / hummingbird's dart— / above your tumbling bones. Desire.
Desire / is praying seven times / daily. My open palms. / We're

always learning / to look. The girl / touches wings, expecting / to wake
the butterflies / instead she learns: how quickly / the body pushes you
out. Unhinge the jaw, / breath-slipped through / tooth constellation.

Unbraiding / the holy. Unlearning / each hymn. Can / you love
the body / as your childhood / ragdoll? Nutshell / candlelit heart
against / yours, binding desire / turning her life / in the lock.

Loving my tiny girl / shouldn't be / such a world burning. / O, my bony
longings. / From the car / the mother watches / the child laboring
under heavy backpack. / Sometimes / the mother enjoys / the struggle.

The mother / remembers her grandfather / drowning runts / pig's cloven
legs butterflying / under the water. Why / can we choose / who lives &
who / doesn't? / A body's a hard / thing to save / when the mother

can't forgive herself / when the girl / wants the mother / to enfold her
again, so much / wanting / no one can tell / the difference between
arrival & departure. / Because I'm the girl / the mother / the drowned.

Tell Me How You Understand Vanishing Point

When we folded / the asphodels away / Prussian blue eggshells / aching

rose thorns / labeled saintly ephemera / when we've cataloged / violet

gloam birds / when we surrender our honeymoon / *now he's inside my*

body & now what. / We don't recall / the future. We learn / to escape

the body / scented heartbeat tangerine / in collar bones. / I wish I could

stay / this young / fly, owl to bruised stars, / in a city on the sea / bathing

my body, you / know the heart's great works / forgiving the need to be

happy / intimate hibiscus, weeping / this mouth lost / in chartreuse. / Our

dead rabbit's / fur dusted behind the couch, / children's teeth hidden

in my drawer. I / hear, *Oh mama*. A river gushes. / I let it. If you / return

to this room / inside me, I'll wait. / Canopy of cherries / at the beginning

of a decorous century. / Here, we stay young. / We turn the calendar

to sunflower season's / brief stand, shadow / on the universe's lip. / Log

church glittering in a shower / of hail. A pig / dies once. / We die over

& again, long before / it happens. It's taken / this long to see / how lavish

this unlimited / now. The escape / backward homeless plunge / off

the balcony / red nightdress floating / this planet a delight / we remember

fondly / in the next world.

Part III

For now you are still / just a word: but / the time is not far / when you will namelessly / unperceived / shine once / again.
—Franz Wright

Notes: Gratitude for Still Being Alive

Yet, the ripped body, cleaned skull. Or an unutterable fluttering
—is a white fir a statue, a girl picking the Lord's flowers without

mercy? This shadow, azure horse ridden by my grandmother's ghost?
O God, who'll be with us until the end of the age. For some of us,

an insomniac night unfurls mazes of poppies inside our brains
—or a wall painted to look like gardens, never destroyed

under ice. I thought I never could love you as much as I loved Venice.
Tamarind bird of my heart, will God's hands close me out?

In the City of Water, arms outstretched, pigeons landed on my shoulders
& hands for seed. I never pretended I could speak for the dead.

Yet, with September's moon, the grape & the fig ready. Bats knit
the firmament into a wild dusk. A blizzard of voices stir up

within my ribs, a language not mine. If I can make every bright
plague a prayer, or constant raise of the body's animal music, if sleep's

a cradle song for nightmares, can we stop our canter toward death?
Dymphna, saint of our anxieties, the poet asks, what can't be mended?

Between water & morning, bone & field, the dead unlock an apocalypse.
Somewhere, Dymphna's father murders her over & over. See how

my one life diverges to other, unexpected lives. Poems will never raise
the dead the way you desire. Yet we still have the sorrows

my daughter says fly as fairy nightingales to land on my backbone.

Fiat Lux

& a cardinal's red burst on the swaying feeder, my son's belly laughter
at seeds flying onto snow what keeps me—

The violins we hear in the winds of winter, before flowers return
to their work—

What keeps me here, the kinds of light: momentary blue, the lift
of water-glint into heavens as a star shedding petals—

YouTube videos of controlled forest burning, black smoke crackling
as clouds of flies, but also clusters of cherries

on the branch, this gift—

How I Learned to Forgive a Good Man

How do I turn my skin gold, how do I keep a man who doesn't want
to be held? When my small son cups our old cat's skull in his hands,
I say, *be careful*, though I know how thick this tiny cranium is, 29
different bony parts. I want him to be a man who doesn't want a woman
for what she can give: baby, turkey dinner, lit kitchen. Our histories
        are uncertain, retold

from mouth to mouth. I always thought a good man was hard to find
as Flannery said. If you did find one, he'd leave eventually. Husband
gave me a wedding ring inscribed with *only you*. Do we hide banish-
ment, a woman fleeing her city, hair clouded in night shade.
Grandmother wished her name was Gloria, not Wanda, ever-lasting
        traveler. Listen, you can't

go back. Everything's changed. Husband can be taken. Or he can't.
It depends whose serpent-shaped lips speak. The 19th century wore
jewelry painted with lovers' eyes—easier to be watcher & watched.
Our secret rooms. My words mound in Husband's ashy bed.
Have you seen medieval altarpieces, teenage blue-hooded Mary
        kneeling with the angel, agreeing

to bear a God who builds microchimeric bodies, so
part of me lives in my son's brain, his leg, no matter where he hides.
If I die, part of me will still live. & Mary's son died & came back &
I want to live forever. I want to hear the prayer under the fruiting prayer,
the impossible prayer still being written. I want to believe in Husband's
        love, but I'm a poet

wearing a blessed scapular. The phenomena of ectoplasm emanating
from a seer's mouth makes sense to me. We're parts of each other.
We're cracked. Mary is like no other. When what they mean is
hysteria's stench & moan. What I mean is, please love me.
Like no other, Husband could unearth my heart, while looking
          into my floating fields.

I saw what we had made, child quotidian & fashioned by
the divine, animal child who prays to St. Francis to keep birds safe.
Is his (my) body also a tabernacle? There are still men with torches.
What's there to forgive? Husband says he won't leave. He says.
The sound
          of day's end,

it's only my son praying. Even now the prayer knocks.
Wake me when.   When I've arrived.

Locutions

Even if you were to slay me, I would hope in you.
      —St. Padre Pio of Pietrelcina

The branches go numb / The monks peel apples / How we age between
this dusk & the next / They leave a scar, because everything / Haven't
we always been seekers / Let me translate for you / This suffering isn't
a punishment / Your soul needs threshing / You can't stay at the base
of the cross / My head shearing / hush-distant hills / Ride into the fire
Don't leave Him / in His agony / The timeless ones / make noise around
you / the holier you are / Knock once to enter / Test every spirit / There
are no hidden doors / to our beatific otherworld / We promise you an
incorrupt body / Starlings rising above stalks / Do you believe / holiness
transforms / you into God / We are made / Water / We scatter / We
riddle / Seven sheep / lost in the cold / We are the dream / you're
dreaming / We believe in the night / Stay in the boat / The storm is yours
Don't doubt / We're here / Keep your eyes / on the eastern skies / Detach
from / this Earth / It's difficult / to be a saint / But it's not impossible
God can do the impossible / The boat moves / slowly / The boat / under
stars / The voices that change / how you walk this world / aren't yours
We wait / for you / until you've arrived / You aren't lost / in our dream
singing

In the Silence After the Other Driver T-Boned Our Car, I Looked in the Rearview Mirror to See if My Children Were Alive

If I'm not dead, it feels as if I am, waking into a haze: this memory
  through leaves turning to mirage. Because there was a hawk,

his heart circling in a slow metronome as glass prismed into our
  hair. You inhabited a lost country I can never remember—

within me, one I'm sick for—there's no returning. Because I thought
  I'd never be a mother—that desire never pitting in my gut

as a calm gravity—no glory in planting tiny bones—fingers my ribcage's
  marginalia. A statue of a Madonna on a lawn beyond. My heart's

sad tap dance—what predawn dreams in the womb, me leading
  my daughter to a field where a white mare dozed, her foal

lifting its head toward my child who saw something of herself—their
  newness that's already waning—a knotting together that prepared

them for disassembling—it's been like waiting for a ghost—I'm holy,
  winded, full of panic—I'm tired of being in a body—yet I lived,

lived—if there was a way to turn my bone broth to light because living
  this way—head knocked this way, brain bruised—because all

I can do is bend and pick my children as daisies—place them
      behind my ears—these days I feel like I'm walking

to the world's edge—when I look over—my children shine—
      when the glass prismed—when they realized bodies could break—

when my head hit—when my shoulder blades knocked loose—when
      what I wanted—flight, to hold their tiny skulls in my arms—when

I think I'm no longer a mother—a mother who doesn't have the chance
      to walk back—to hold a baby in the middle of a field—to say,

my bones are in you—if I go to the sky—if I, if I—I can't bear this,
      to die.

The Shape of Disappearing

In a bed of succulents, I dream I'm barren. Dreaming

my son into a white horse. Jangle of shoehorns.

Of eternity, a world no one can own. Woman lifting

a jug, a puff of flour at the bottom. This house,

where everything's familiar, but foreign. In a bed

of succulents, his eye's tender pool. I'm unlike women

who save rhapsodic things to pass down: wedding bone

china sets, silver, scrapbooks of faded summers. Mountain

that outlives me. Why traveling only toward the light

breeds another drowning. Sleepers in your garden,

choiring marrow-glow—who's to say the baffling lantern

I see in the dark isn't me, coming for me? Feathering

ill wind. Remembering you telling me to *go under*

—part otherworldly, shimmer of blue tracks across snow.

Because our bodies can't stop haunting each other. Crooked

flowering crown, horsefly swarm. Tiny tracks flighted,

the opal-veiled virgin in the medieval painting's middle

distance, where falcons return, then vanish. Why living

on heaven's brim isn't living. Watch as I grow to love

what's taking me away.

A Dream Where My Father Walks on Water, After He Decided to Burn His Childhood Photos

He entered my nights. Like a falcon, a steed, sure of himself, but also
softly, a dove landing
on balsam. Oscillations of grief. There are oranges, sunflowers, men
returning from the sea,
loves gone into the ground. Shouldn't prayer show me I'm alone
in the world

& not alone enough? He turns to a luminous school of fish in the Seine.
The water is light.
The future, the color of tea. In Vietnam, a junkyard rat bit his arm. Elvis
still playing on the radio.
At the top of a mountain in Saigon, under bone stars, he wished
for cherries, the scent

of wet bark. He draws graffiti behind my eyes. *Orange orchard. Travel
light. Sarcophagus.* Unshrouds
his body to show me his operation scars. The cornea from a dead man.
He wanted
to be a carp to outswim his future. He knew he'd never see his home
again. His face is my face.

He wanted to be the gray tornado he watched rupturing houses
on the next street, rather than
go inside for another beating. He still dreams of Vietnam. Now I dream
of war, but without
sound. But smoke in my father's hands. The lunar eclipse. I dream
of the soldier

threatening to kill him with a 12-inch knife. But that night the soldier
died from a lightning
strike, his body crumpled on the knife on a hill. My father says if he
was killed,
I wouldn't have been born. God's country drowns in my father. My
father shows me the place

his feeding tube went in, the shallow under his ribs.

I Still Don't Believe in the Beauty
of Forgiveness

God, we spend our whole / lives persevering / long winter stars scalding
us / as if heaven's a place / real as the corner diner / alight all night
where I enter / easily even as a sinner / hungering for eggs / over easy
& devour them. / Let's cover this early on: / You've already forgiven
the despicable things / I'll do. / Fire-starter, fire-water. / Fireball of my
nights, / the last blackout / last eclipse. / Except I keep waking / up here.
Fanciful, keeping to rituals / black coffee at 6 am / despite a blazing
hangover. / I wish I was never. / Born catastrophe, moss in / my teeth.
Can a spirit / hide in a plum? In / a bird? Deserted / city? They told me
so many people / in these rooms / want to welcome me in / this glass
hour. I used to say / it's not my fault / I was born blackhearted / death
wish in my skull. / These sober saints / who believe in / fruited
sufferings to come. / We're lacerated / with an intimate thorn
from the crown. / Bedclothed in firelight, / Christ's memory howls
in my haunted / room. Lord, do / you still know me / after all I've done?
When we took / the baby lionhead rabbit / to go to sleep / because
the cancer pushed / her eye out the socket / what undid me was / her
golden-white hair / tufting across the floor / as if she hadn't died.
This is how I understand / death: I'm here now / & you're still there.
If you awaken, you'll hear my creak. / Nothing left but God's voice,
Please—if the body's a door / a well hole / a bridge—I've tried to cross
from this body, / a sacred wound left / as if God lives on / in witness
trees, in my mud. / As if God lets / me live on, eternal / the past, present
& future / the old me / lit, lonely & my own sad / light colliding
with a new me / irradiated walking so close / to this side of paradise.

When I sit / in a pew / thinking of every awful / wrong I've done to another person / I know the giving / back will never end. / I told myself until / I can forgive myself. / Until I fold back / to a child / who can see morning glories / with new eyes. / But no, my God / who's always there shows me only / he can remove / the steely stench. / All you need to do is ask. / Ask how to turn / your life holy. / It's already done. / The light coming from centuries / ago is just now arriving / on time.

O Wise Mother, Your Body Always the Door, Turning Heaven Back to the World

ephemeral	ectoplasms	irradiant
shimmering	darkheart	infinite
rapt	infiltrate	ensnare
encircle	entrap	beguile
enshrine	invoke	ethereal
ecstatic	withering	levitation
shrouded	sainted	luminous
sublimation	incandescent	supernatural
levitation	revelation	familiar

Littlest Bones

As a child, my mother asked me: Will you die for Christ? Hickory
incense—when I first held my nine-weeks-early son, briars broken,
lamentations, I thought to clothe him in my own skin. My dispersal
into a flock, a swarm, a gallery of winged stars—how easy to imagine
I could die for him. I admit it: I didn't want to live without him.
Heaven's a place—full of swans, of milk. Before it ever happens,
you make a choice. Littlest bones. His bones parted metal chimes,
black calligraphy backlit through parchment. This wind. Imagine
José Luis Sánchez del Río rebel-fighting in the Cristero War.
Delicate skeleton, seeded to grow 12 pairs of ribs. Let's say the boy's
captured. The soldiers tell him to renounce God. José's mother drew
tiny star maps (yes, the heavens) on his soles. When I first touched
my son, my mother said, *if he doesn't live, he'll be with Christ.* Shiny,
silver fished xylophone waiting in his nursery. My gossamer son.
Little bones, you'll bear my son to the end of his life. My secret
ossuary. José's soles knifed off when he wouldn't deny. Imagine
your child's martyrdom. Your own. A choice some of us were born
to make. Like José, who walked on holy-ghosted bone feet, in love,
in desperate love, shouting *Long Live Christ the King, Christ My King,*
soldiers shooting, missing till they didn't.

After Not Drinking Anymore

The fire I've zealously / cast myself into year / after year isn't
supernatural at all. / This fire smells / of death & seared skin / of a soul
gored. / This fire isn't ecstatic— / doesn't levitate or bilocate / like a
departing saint / setting this world / on an otherworldly fire. / This fire
isn't / a sacramental the way / you imagine / my heart gurgling
with the wrong loves. Yet / God is inside & out / filling this organ
with so / much pressure / it's a conch shell drinking / in all the ocean.
Today could be / the last day / of my life— / or yours. / I came back
to tell you it's OK to come / back as you are / charred or smoking
or dazzling. But / I won't take myself / out. This fire scorched / in me
the will / to live illumined. / Because you're dust & lichens / a flame
at the base / of your heart / I love you. / You're a wind / a darkness
singing, birds / signaling to each other. / My body isn't yours / so there
are no words / to explain the act / of dying. / A flame darkens / these
silences. / This life is alternately / living & leaving / over again
toward a perfect end / waiting inside you / a pomegranate / containing
many seeds / of your days. / At a certain point / I had to choose life
this side of heaven. / The weighty chaos / of overdosing— / riding fiery
adrenaline— / stopped. Then / the ineluctable fragrance / of God
billowing in spring rain / also in the terrible darkness / of blackouts.
There's still time to love / the ones who left you / find the ones
to forgive countryless you, / find your face reflecting / in winter's
ice pond / your knees kneeling / in snow. / The dark compassing
the cold burning so / like the boundless fire / that consumed you
so you can be safe / everywhere.

73

Lux Brumalis

I can't look at the sky's orange light over the color of ashes now
without weeping. The fiery sparks among snow showers aren't
an asymmetry of traveling souls. The lioness sun

drops. My father sees out of a dead man's cornea. Drops an army
of golden doves. The loveliness of a gladiola as it withers.

My uncle cast a branch through my father's eye, an accident playing
soldiers before they shipped off to Vietnam after Christmas, plane
whirring in a blue splendor. We almost didn't go

to the beach that summer, sky full of unrest.
Our last day, a freak lightning storm killed a teenage lifeguard
waving everyone off the beach. Garlands of flowers

at the bottom of her chair, the only visible sign. Her body's ghostsong,
if you could hear it, among terns' crying. We return here in a blurring

haze, my daughter pointing at translucent horses
in the waves, sky tinged yellow—the beauty of shadowing, as my father
thins & grows older in winter light, reflecting inside mother-of-pearl
shells, twilight in his one eye.

Part IV

My past, O Lord, to Your mercy; my present,
to Your love; my future to Your providence.
                    —St. Padre Pio of Pietrelcina

Locution I: We are more wretched than the animals

My son broke / open my body / extravagant thrush, eyes / of a
horse, feathers furling / in ordinary light. / My crevasse—
brine darkening— / a cauldron I couldn't see / within to look
for him. Honeyed thrums, / his wings / forelock moving wisps
in amniotic waters / in aurora / borealis his gleaming / heart
gallop. In his / presence. / The body of the son / the sun.
I knelt, / morning light / quiet ocean / the world blowing / past.
Listen— / breaking bread / a shearing / the body of Christ
torn asunder / suturing my body / back after my son / broke
his wings / his smear. / We kept a vigil / his first nights. / No
candlelight. Thirsting foal / who can't stand. / A bird winding
through time. / A boy learns / to hold a gun. / A boy learns
to lay down / his life for others. / My son / scattered me
in pieces / glass / parables / aromatic salts / red sky. / Two
together / is a miracle. / It's me talking / in silence. / Walled
in a city. / Lord, let me / have poems / in my afterlife. / My fault:
not wanting / to leave my son / for God / who comes after me
dazzling sun's body / break me / break me / from deadening
break me / as I bloom / from my heir.

Locution II: This is a love that kills

A swallow's wings splayed / on the barn floor / crucified.
Do sun-drifting bones / remember the whole / of the bird?
Looking back / through its flight / the eyes that saw / a whole
world / in joy / cloud-wandering / baby in slick / yellowed
afterbirth / spine glowing wonder. / If this is love / if this
is pain / verdigris on the heart / if this is a paean / I could
memorize his first cry / & now can't remember / the parting
of our birth-marked / bodies. A primordial / mourning overcast
over-laid with Gregorian / chants my son born / two months
early / my son. / Not a king / we build a tomb / for as he reigns
spirit of ferocious / sun. My body / a door / a death-gate
if his heart / his cloistral before-life / lingering / in shadow,
in spectral / waters. Phantasmagoria— / where we have met
before / or after? / In penance / in tendrils / of fire, bees'
gold incantations / we witnessed / his smoke-breath / incensing
his skull / emerging. My glory / of not groaning when / I
released him / my seafern hand / hymnbook / that stillness
cracked / his voice box / he / parting.

Locution III: A blackened flower among thorns

Call it premonition / call us / call it knowing / in rain,
discerning. Sage sticks divining / with the body / not metal
rods / a woman made of water, / knowing with bone / marrow.
Push / harder to push / him into my now. / This second sight
a gift / the stone always / in my shoe. / In violet summer
a girl hitchhikes. / Drinking chai. / The distances between
our bodies. / A cafe at Venice Beach. / Sun that wouldn't end
its flighted hunt. / Brown sugar swirling / in my mug. / Hunger
like chiffon / his parchment skin / the color of medieval
effigies, stone faces / blanched in cathedral light / streaming
shine of clairaudience / as if I heard: / *I made it / to paradise.*
I never dreamed / him before / his heart started. / Yet, he stopped
moving three times. / I dreamed birthing / him still. / My son,
in sage / flowers in large green hands. / There's a book / of two
worlds: / Before. After. / His name / means in the memory
of God before / he existed. This tiny / nightingale / my
remembrance / my third eye couldn't see / my hands' span
on my stomach / linea nigra from pelvis / to ribcage / the dark
line reading / it's a boy / with wingbones / in light / sorcery
untranslatable / still.

Locution IV: I weep for this world

So many ways to break / open / but invisible. / These
translucencies I know / spindling / a pulse / a toothache
no one sees / the impressions / these old / blackouts
migraines looking through / shattered glass / the body held
down by a man / a brown horse going by / honey / orchard
I walk / because all / the difficult days / cinnamon liquor's
resin / trapping me. / Salt, stars. / The sound of the tea
kettle. Clink of spoons / slowing it all down. / Plums.
Nettles. Brambling / in my gut. Start / of the baby / my son.
A bliss. Bleed. / A moment from now / a week / a month.
Incommensurable / time / to grow / his bones. / His irises
rising / his fists / his gleam. / A thick root / the world
growing brighter. / The wind rushing / up the slope. / Pines
more alive / sweet sapped / than I recall. / A stranger singing
beyond this line. / I'm taken. I / remember / my grandfather
playing / the violin / the squeak / the disharmony's rage
of joy. / In Van Gogh's starry / night / I still lose / myself
heaving body / no longer a straight line. / There's no face
like his. / I became huge / a globe / with new languages.
Yet, he flies from me.

Locution V: He is the law of crows

Which is to say / one hundred or more / crows gather / when
one dies. / None touch / the final glisten of black / feathers,
foot or eye / earth-bound now. / Spreading our hair / in honey
over the door / guard us in / our city of sleep. / We assemble
the crib hang the mobile of blue- / yellow birds' / fanciful
flights. / I wish for a vampire / killing kit / antique box
with a bronze crucifix, holy / water, a hammer / stakes
the face of my Lord fragmenting / my rainy / night into
feathers / oil the remnants / of nostalgia / the dangers
when I sifted / through my grandfather's / black-and-white
photos / of Europe in 1944 / as he crossed countries
as a soldier / with his camera / sheep next to a bombed
house, a child / holding an apple / her eyes forever / full
of loneliness / as when I / spent summers / at the lake / near
Otter Island. / The desolation / of not fitting / with other
girls / but still the lap / of gray water / as I lay in / a musty
hammock / that comforting / sound never left / my body
rocking in slanted / sun / smell of marsh grass / the lull
of loons / a time where / I could still / belong. Which
is to say / should we stop / calling them a murder? / They
harbinger. / Candle-blown-out. / They cry / loudly / as babies
calling in the dark / to float on water.

Locution VI: Bleeding is burning is survival

My grandmother / bled in secret / strange / natural wonder
her remote / mother never explained. / There's a glacier / faraway
that bleeds gruesome crimson / saltwater's ancient / basin without
light, heat / or air / what we need / to thrive / the water too / salty
to freeze / so when it pierces / tiny fissures / in the ice / cascading
bloody / into the Antarctic. / My favorite music / to play / (survive)
in my vintage / fireball red Trans Am: / heavy metal / coppery riffs
caustic smell / my first bleed / that taut tether / to the feminine
my '80s biker jacket / for a dude / made me infamous / in high
school / squeak of seams / pungent petrol / smell deep / in old cow
hide / but maybe we all / need a second skin an intercession:
O Holy God / our world's disappearing / there's no guarantee
I'll have an eternal / abode / lamentations & / Revelation's rivers
of blood or the calcifying / Tanzanian lake / that turns / animals
& birds / to stone / feathers filigreed / by natron / in the water
silver over gray wing / bones & ribs / like bodies mothers & beasts
frozen forever / in Pompeii ash / our migration suspended.

Part V

*come celebrate / with me that everyday /
something has tried to kill me / and has failed.*
—Lucille Clifton

Morning Prayer

Fog blows, trails left from salt-covered stars' edges

String thick thread through red & yellow peppers, scent of wet dirt

Cupped hands raised to first light, damp & earth-clinged

Fire ember pops, last to die as night's excesses of love

Spine curves like a swan's neck—its wings moving through moss

& shadows

At your feet, my lips

My hands, soil on palms, are ancient butterflies

O, release the dawn, the scent of apples, of rain

Diverging

When I want another time / but also now / we take the fireball red
legendary Trans Am / through the deserted Pine Barrens. / It's turning
the years / back two decades / the shift / & heft of this car's doors
creased leather seats / smelling old oil & yellow wax / my biker
jacket from the '80s / molded to some dude's body / but also mine.
The car, sunset's aftermath. / Maybe I'm afraid / where this year
pulls me / rough foamy tide's empty / cans & seaweed / replacing
what I remember. / Feeding cardinals / winter grasses / & snow
their red chatter still alive / because we were there. / This car—
the body— / a strange porthole / for seeing / the world / as it is,
as it was / a finch turning inside another finch / my grandmother
who's gone / still hungry & awake / somewhere. / Girth of God
shadowing my house. / Trans Am in the rain. / We parked by a tiny
church & its headstones / next to an abandoned / house clairvoyant
among the pines & cloud / cover hymning songs I've / never heard
& never will again. / The rapt question / when we shut / the lights:
Today, / how have you / prepared for your death? / I can't recall
the exact / tactility of my fingers / touching an 1864 grave / marker's
grit & moss. / But still, I know / the dampness / entering my arm
bones / as a way to mark time / warning that home never / stays
the same. / It's always floating— / moving on bird feet. / When
you sleep / I touch your palm's fate / lines. It's difficult / for me
to explain / why loving you / is dangerous / as driving the Trans Am
in freezing rain / toward disaster / also a reward. / I can't recall
a future where / I've stopped caring / for you. / Or where you never
lived at all. / Where / I can't tell / you how I've / broken things
again. / We can't go back / to how it was / when you were a stranger
to me / when your body's / a new land / my womb still empty. / I

remember Caravaggio / shadows in Paris catacombs / on skulls, ribs holding / centuries of raspberry hearts. / Golden light from the shaft above. / Like tiger lilies falling.

Lost Things Keep Appearing

32,000 years ago, my husband texts me,
      ice trapped an Artic ground squirrel.
            That might have been the end of a world,
                  but scientists grew a flowering plant

from fossil fruit in her stomach. *Should we*
      have a third child? I carry DNA from any child
            I've grown, I read online, so I'm never
                alone in my body. What haunts

our house, our daughter asks—she heard
      a man mutter, *hook, line &—*& what? A horseman
            burying a red foal in the pasture's gloaming?
                This guy, his 7-year-old boy was shot.

I can't talk about him out loud. My husband
      only cries for children. A father who loses his son
            hews his body into a rowboat, creaked ribs opening
                to the son's light—it's gone, gone, gash left

as if he birthed him. Is the man still a daddy,
      our daughter asks, if he left his little girls behind?
            Let's play under the house, she sings, *let's, let's all*
                us ghosted girls play ring around dusty roses.

There's no one to teach us to die well. There's no one
      to teach us to let bodiless children go. *This guy*
            kept reminders, secrets, after donating everything else,
                baseball cap shaped to a tiny skull hanging

in the shed, baby teeth boxed & netted
      bag of sunlit hair in his desk. How harsh
            mourning is: Does he say at night, *Son, come home.*
                Whose voice does he expect to hear? Where's

home now? *He thought about killing himself,* joining
　　　　his son—he'd open his heart, emerging a stranger.
　　　　　　The stars loom the little boy a blanket, hymning him
　　　　　　　　in the cinnamon dark. The father holds

his body as spruce boat, still on dawn's water,
　　　　waiting for a heron to land on his prow, together
　　　　　　We're lashed where we'll never return
　　　　　　　　a lifetime of small hands waving.
　　　　　　　　　　Yes, come.

Yesterday's Gutted Girl

When you open your mouth   for food   & broth   for praise   for, *oh*
help me   all that's holily lonely   she'll pour in salt. If   you revere

the Lord's five   wounds, there's   land so massive   divine &
bone.   I didn't slip my   hand into his side.   I didn't ask

when a body's safe   to stay alive in   & didn't   un-conjure mothers
hiding when babies   cry under bright   hills.   Where souls press

all our longing   against rusted rain-   dotted windows.
I don't tell   my daughter a school   mate died. His body's

tiny bungalow.   Sundown's quieting   bones. Later, I explain
the avocado-pit   tumor. *But what an immense   land he gets*

now   she tells me.   Someday, her grief   a memory:
nightingale frozen   under ice.   For the mother's   puddling

reflection, ghost   animal in spruce.   Bees descended.   Still,
the trees' singing.   Pray   for humility—the mice   our

traps   caught,   hunger snapped   their necks.   Can we
walk   under sunlight spinning   through the garden   gate

back into   our olden days?   Which is me   harmonizing
chaos.   Landscape   in which God's   everything. Where

you earn   no more glory.   If pain   looks like radiant
city ruins. Yesterday's   gutted girl.   Oh.   But we begin again.

My mother told   me my name.   The door shut   before I
looked   back & met her   quiet eyes,   every girl in me

leaping, my   cast-iron darkness   gold & jumbled   feverish wings
perched on   purgatory's   coast: The wind.   A thirsty child.

Red dress, always   unable to reach   the bird bath, God's
resurrected nightingale   singing until   it's time   it's time

to come home.

Lux Aeterna

My grandmother's phantom city whitewashed by a heartsick sea.
Maybe there was no water, but I heard its gushing heave when she
storied the Old World, a psalm out of time. Stone

houses, corn poppies & baby's breath, the heavy scent of beef & cabbage
outside. The Lord's hand on it all. I try on *surrender* & *specter*.
Shouldn't prayer carry the weight of meeting God
for the first, real time—

the way snow returns & I walk into His face?

My daughter fills every silence with humming, where I hear peasant
songs among chaffinches, old women in checkered dresses still making
duck's blood soup. The ground frozen in Advent.
Their steps sounding on the stairs.

My grandmother's body stout as a houseboat, illuminated by candles
my mother lights at the side altar for her safe passage—through
the needle's eye—

even as evening fades, as the gardener puts away his shovel,
as our tea cools.

Novena for When My Son Says He Doesn't Want
to See Spirits

Protect this boy who slid into a well-oiled world,
glossy bluegill nine weeks too soon, a touch of the mystic—

there wasn't time to wipe the slick, the third eye's loneliest
country from his mind. Being haunted passes down:

I know how we're orphaned outside the mirrored gate,
finger bones looped in its lock. Holy waters, sinking shining

stones. My son knows déjà vu, already seeing his next-life as short
smartphone videos: laughing as he throws soft bread slices

to swans, their glisten alive before the sun ever hits feathers.
Star of the Sea, in this month of the eclipse, crickets lose their

way, the book of nights opening in the penumbra of my heart's
unlit church. Will there be a new heaven and earth for us, full

of small comforts? Goldenrod, applewood, mistletoe, butter,
a golden crow & one malevolent fruit in my quiver.

My young son doesn't understand the arrows that fly by night,
or the hooded apparitions appearing even in daylight's song.

Despite eternity, we inherited one form of destruction. Body,
a river for the living and dead to depart in and out. A tea kettle's

familiar hymning whistle, the rabbits' toenails clicking on our wood
floors: Among the mundane, we think of Lazarus who died twice,

of Padre Pio who can't stop returning to sick rooms, a spirit sent
to heal our bodies during a plague. Woman Clothed With the Sun,

how far is it by boat, by ecstatic wing?

Meditation Excerpt: Mater Dolorosa

Again, the plague season returns. Again, horses live, & they die. Locusts descend, devour, disperse. All ashes. I watch you in the fields, drifting in & out of hinterland mists. A brindle foal learns to stand. Three times during my second pregnancy, we thought we lost our son—once in Gettysburg's bee-buzzed peach orchard. How does love fill all our losses? If we're silent, still the stones will ring. Mater Dolorosa, you never ask why I don't stop talking about suffering. You know darkness ripens darkness. We wear the Black Scapular as a history of your seven sorrows. Each dagger a flaring immensity through your heart, a kind of fanged animal. And yet you are so human: Losing your child in the temple. My fountain. Meeting him on the way to Calvary. My fawn. His agony as he hung beneath an eclipsed sky. My shepherd. Watching a soldier strike a spear into his heart after he died. Mother Mary, I watch you hold your lacerated son, as I wait among your feathery lumen. We talk of paradise. Your mortal body transfiguring to shining immortal woman. We talk of love. I remove my body like a cloak & rise.

Noctuary

Painted wings

knifing all this shimmer. I'm caught
        here, yet this can't last. Bones sprouting

      among grasses,

a midwife hanged for lost children. Exposed
        lamb sliding out, eyes still shut. Behold, horse

      teeth. Slow

      hum of an old dog's heart. An elegy that saints the mother.
      Another father smashing his daughter's

      favorite record.

      What happened is always happening somewhere.
      How what I've done today—wrote a few

      discordant lines

—a woman's face, mosaicked in Pompeii—counts
        as more than marginalia. How a magnolia

flower still

floats in a bowl. Tell me a story of how
        prayer stopped a drowning. Honeysuckle,

ram-trampled.

Tell me why abstaining from meat saves another
          from dying. Tell me a story about an aloof

bird coven.

A hunter kneels in a field. Ritual of summer noon, full sun.
          Our hands make shadow girls shear

over the lawn. These

          smallest, insidious kingdoms.

Ouija of the Heart

One night, stumbling drunk—
with no destination except anywhere-but-here
—I walked down the foggy road.
I discovered a doe hit by a car,

still alive. I knelt next to her
in the amber light. I touched her neck.
Leaned toward her black eye,

shared a last breath, the color
of peonies. A type of planchette,

pointing away from my death.

i

Some of us, born
to leave the earth martyrs—
names destined for the hagiography.

You won't know
if you're marked until
it happens
but you must decide—
Viva Cristo Rey, or burn.

I see the faces of the dead, in rings of mist. Maybe they long again for
a body: to hold a teacup, sit on the back porch

fix everything they regret.

I've heard you won't receive
the grace to die until it's time—
yet my daughter said, *I'm ready to be a soldier for Christ.*

i

I thought I could confess the nights of blacking out & waking up.
    Yet, despite receiving absolution, I can't forget fragmented
flashes. Pushed down on my back by man trying to get my pants off

in the street. The candles spreading fire that almost engulfed my
    room. Taking a knife to my wrist & cutting a cross into it.

i

Wrapped bones in the crypt, girl saint,
we tell your story over & over, so
many apocryphal versions we don't know
what you did to become winged.
Some of us would kill to unlock

salvation. As daylight fades, my God,
watch my bed, let dreams depart
    & phantoms fly, night's offspring.

i

What I want: to change my life. What I want: to die in love with God.

i

With & without my daughter. Without, my ankles still submerged by
    honeysuckle she leafed over—with, her hands tangled in my fingers &
tiger's eye & lapis lazuli rings she won't let go. With, her hummingbird
light bones crossed over my legs—without, the scent of rose hips & thorns
remind me of her precise fingers.

Without, the house lets go the light bound up in its beams—with, her hands
hands mixing petals in a bowl of water. With, she prays to warrior Michael
the Archangel to submerge Satan in the sea again—without, if I
could be anything in the world, the mother lets go all the pain
(the subsuming) as if they don't matter.

Without, I light red candles to Our Lady of Częstochowa to protect her—
with, my hand on her hand, touching a miracle. With, if I could be
anything, the mother who knows she dies, the pains of growing
a girl will matter to enter heaven—

without, a gold-plated head reliquary, holding my severed neck, its
quiver, its life.

i

I imagine my children ripening in another woman's hands. My son adds

and it was to every story's end. My daughter claps to rewrite

a tale. They ask my husband if they'll be sad like me. I name it demon.

Leveling. But a kind of grace to meet death & refuse it.

i

I was never a teenage saint like you Maria, Maria Goretti—he penetrated
your thorax & the pericardium.
He stabbed your heart's left auricle, your left
lung. The abdomen. 18 times. The small intestine
& the iliac. 18 stabs, Maria.

But what sainted you more than saving your virginity,
forgiving your rapist before you died.

i

Our Lady, Undoer of Knots, I entrust into your hands this everlasting
knot that robs my peace.

Meditation Excerpt: Change Me, O Ghost

My God, why does the bruised flower inside me cry *open*? Shape-shifter birds, my daughter called skyward: Flock of Holy Ghosts, can I fly with you? She's my compass toward paradise. My human will, the only door for evil spirits to enter. Holy the purity of animals in forests & pastures, breath hymning outside my ordinary house. Your grace alchemized into a luminous dove. Your tongue is useful. Tell me, how did I look before your first grief? Heaven's language never passes away. Bless the age to come, where we name suffering: fire's harmony. Yet, we live between the countries of the dead. Change me, O Ghost, your somnolent voice in the air. Listen: It's not simple to be a mother in this world. It's easier to wake alone & grind the coffee. But holy their slumbering cries. Holy this world, not the world. Holy the Ghost's memory, where I've lived for all time and no time. My heart, his perch. Ghost, in storms and tsunamis. My Ghost, who lives in plagues, in accord. My Ghost, who nurses children, who says, show them mercy in your everydayness. The beginning, the end.

Little Candle in the Coming Rain

When my son stepped on a tiny toad, crushing it to warm ooze,
he's inconsolable, the splay of legs reflecting his prayer hands:
God, can't you bring him back?

Restart the heart. Reassemble his spine's nine vertebrae? My son
learned he can kill, but not raise the dead. Years later, three boys
will hold him down at summer camp

beyond the trees, scratching his neck, forcing him to say, *You're the best,*
the best, before letting him up into a changed world.
O, we're entrusted with other lives.

We want to believe we'll always be loved. During the pandemic,
I clumsily cut his hair, leaving scalp patches in the buzz cut
—his small shoulders rounded

in front of me, hands cupping a blue Transformer, making robot
sounds under his breath. My son will say he deserved to be jumped,
since he na-na-na'd these kids

one too many times. He won't go back to the camp
where he should have made friends, ate hot dogs, cannon
balled into the cold pool.

Nothing stays forever, as he'll learn he can get back up, red shirt
torn—but he wants to know if someone can kill him, like he did
the toad. As a mother, I can't shelter my son

from what comes to devour him—sweaty hands around his neck,
poison ivy under their nails. But there's no earthly love
that undoes. His body lived

in my body, room inside a room. Wilderness
in a wilderness.

Lamp Lighting

I walk a Roman road—where the Lord once appeared, ghost feet rubbed
in salt. *Domine, quo vadis?* To preserve myself my buried hand bones

open into vines of light. My mother says spirit children still cry
for their daddies who don't ever come home & the body lives forever—

severed head hallowed & bowed, striated sinews, fossil honeycombed
with memory somewhere—as when I listened to a bird I can't name,

shelled ocean at a cistern's bottom. In a chapel-under-the-church, a girl
martyr's tomb smells of dust & pears, dust bones, wind vertebrae. Even

after this long, I can smell the Lord on her breath. Still, I hide from him.

      My mother says the Lord
only shows saints his shoulder wound—most secret of gashes. When
the Lord arrives, he'll be silent on dragon feet, claws in—virgins

waiting with lanterns of sweet oil—the medieval artisan, first spindling
colors into rose windows, indulgences ascending him as starlings,

hyacinth wings lined with lead had to find solace in these new iron &
glass bodies light (a way home would pierce) over pilgrims for centuries,

didn't he? My mother says the Lord will always have his nail holes—
how can I ask to be spared from death any longer because even

     in paradise there are reminders of who killed you.

Litany with Outpouring Light

My son says his body's full of honey, jarred, electric bees—

You've asked me, *Have you ever heard a death rattle*—

I've asked back if it's possible to drown inside yourself, without
sighing—

I learned to pray anywhere you can name *home* or *falling leaves* or
falling—

My son, who wouldn't drink my milk, smelled of wet petals—

I buried longing within my pelvis, yet the wide sky opening
in my chest—

He asks: *How long before I burst open with golden flight*—

A parent hardly sleeps & prays in snippets, *I'm the bell, I'm the well
for your worries*—

God, is that you climbing my stairs? Is it the body of the sun—

I find a note my son started writing crumpled under his bed,
Dear Bee King, it's me—

A window to eternity, to remembrance's jar of black seeds waiting—

Crumbs gathered at the bottom of my purse, child of passing time—

Afterlife, afterbirth, after-nights, night from night from wind singing—

I saw you in my dream, falling beside me into another country—

I ask if you heard my death rattle in the dream we shared—

The places we've been together, the places with no names—

I remember living & not living—

The echo of bee wings everywhere I want to be—

About the Author

Nicole Rollender is an accomplished, award-winning poet and writer, with an impressive list of accolades to her name. In 2017, she was recognized as a poetry fellow by the NJ Council on the Arts. She has authored two poetry collections, including *Louder Than Everything You Love* (Five Oaks Press, 2017) and *The Luster of Everything I'm Already Forgetting* (Kelsay Books, 2023), as well as four poetry chapbooks. *Bone of My Bone* won the 2015 Blood Pudding Press award.

Her poetry has earned her numerous prizes and awards, including recognition from *Catholic Literary Arts, Center for Interfaith Relations, Palette Poetry, Gigantic Sequins, CALYX Journal,* and *Ruminate Magazine.*

Nicole's work has been featured in an impressive range of journals, such as *Alaska Quarterly Review, Best New Poets, Ninth Letter, Puerto del Sol, Salt Hill Journal,* and *West Branch.*

She is also the managing editor of *THRUSH Poetry Journal* and holds an MFA in Creative Writing from the Pennsylvania State University.

In addition to her literary writing career, Nicole is the co-founder and CEO of STRANDWritingServices.com.

To learn more about Nicole and her work, visit her website at:

www.nicolemrollender.com